Donated by
Morrison County
Genealogy Society

A Genealogist's Guide to Researching Civil War and Dakota Conflict Ancestors in Minnesota

by Mary Hawker Bakeman

PARK GENEALOGICAL BOOKS

Park Genealogical Books
P O Box 130968
Roseville, Minnesota 55113

Cover credits

Design by Carol Barrett of CRG Digital Design, St. Paul.

The painting *The Second Minnesota Regiment at Missionary Ridge* by Douglas Volk hangs in the Governor's Reception Room at the State Capitol, and is from the collections of the Minnesota Historical Society, St. Paul, MN.

The *Map of the Battle of Gettysburg, Pa., July 1st, 2nd & 3rd, 1863 showing line of battle on P.M. of 2nd* is from the Library of Congress Geography and Map Division, Washington, DC.

The report from Timothy Sheehan about the attack on Fort Ridgely is from *A Compilation of the Official Records of the Union and Confederate Armies*, better known as the "OR." The noise and boom of the well-placed cannonballs by John Jones helped the Indians decide to return to fight again another day.

The portrait of *Major General John Pope* by Matthew Brady is part of the Brady Collection in the Prints & Photograph Division of the Library of Congress. Pope entered the U.S. Military Academy in 1838, at age 16. He commanded the Army of the Mississippi and was successful in opening up the upper half of that river. Pope was sent west to campaign against the Sioux Indians in 1863, where he remained until his retirement in 1886.

The map from the *Official Atlas of the Civil War* shows the route of Sibley's Expedition in 1863 following the Dakota Indians out of Minnesota, and the forts and camps along the way. The camps are named for officers.

The *Rev. James Peet* served as Chaplain to the 50th U.S. Colored Troops. He was recruited by Lt. Col. Robert Donaldson, a member of his congregation in Dakota County and an officer in the 4th Minnesota. His wife Harriet remained in Minnesota with their children. Rev. Peet died in Anoka in 1867. Photo courtesy of the Archives, Minnesota Conference of The United Methodist Church.

Marshall Sherman, a Minnesota Medal of Honor winner, fought at Gettysburg with the First Minnesota, where he is credited with capturing the flag of the 28th Virginia, which still remains in the collections of the Minnesota Historical Society. In 1864, he lost a leg at Deep Bottom Run, near Darbytown, Virginia. He is buried in the Soldiers' Rest at Oakland Cemetery, St. Paul. Bakeman photo.

Library of Congress Control No. 2005905611

ISBN 1-932212-15-9

© 2005, Park Genealogical Books, Roseville, Minnesota

Table of Contents

Introduction 1

Acknowledgements 3

Beginning a Family History Search 5
   The Historical Setting 5
   Federal Census Records 7
      Federal Census Availability 11
   Minnesota State Census 13
   Cemetery Research 13
   The Minnesota GenWeb 14
   Shortcuts. 14
   Minnesota Research Bookshelf. 15

Getting Familiar with Military Terminology 17

Major Repositories of Civil War Information 23
   The National Archives (NARA). 23
      Special National Archives Finding Aids 24
   Civil War Soldiers &Sailors System (CWSS) 24
   Library of Congress (LOC) 25
   The Minnesota History Center 26
      Special MHS Finding Aids. 27
   Minnesota County Historical Societies 27
   University of Minnesota - Wilson Library. 27
   Public and Academic Libraries 28
   "Must Reads" - Minnesota Resources 28

First, Research Your Ancestor 29
Service Records 29
Places to Look 30
Official Government Reports 33
Pensions 34
Compiling a Soldier's Record 39

Second, Research the Unit 43
General References 47
Minnesota References 47

Civilians at Home 53
The Press 53
Refugee Relief 54
Grand Army of the Republic, Department of Minnesota . . 54
Depredation Claims 55

Travel 57

Contact Information 59

Introduction

The role of the State of Minnesota in the Civil War overshadows and exceeds what one would expect of a frontier state. Established in 1858, its prominence during 1861-1865 is unquestioned. When Fort Sumter was fired upon on 12 April 1861, Minnesota's was the first governor to offer to raise a volunteer regiment. The First Minnesota was but one regiment in an army with more than 300 regiments and batteries at Gettysburg, but it played a pivotal role in securing a victory for the Union. Minnesota soldiers marched with Sherman, and some became officers in the newly recruited regiments of freed slaves. The young state definitely made its mark upon United States history.

Fort Snelling, located at the confluence of the Minnesota and Mississippi rivers, had been established in 1820. Fur traders arrived earlier, using the waterways of the Great Lakes to take their pelts to the markets in the east. By 1849 enough settlers had arrived to qualify the Minnesota Territory. The opening of the land for farming over the next decade brought more settlers, from New England, New York, Pennsylvania, Ohio, Illinois and Indiana.

A portion of the Soldiers' Rest at Oakland Cemetery, St. Paul. Slowly deteriorating original markers are are being replaced by new military markers. R.I. Holcombe, though not a Minnesotan at the time of his military service, is the author of many works on Minnesota history. *-Bakeman photo.*

Federal treaties with the Dakota in 1851 and 1858 opened more land to white settlement and created Indian reservations along the upper Minnesota River. With the disappearance of the buffalo once hunted by the Dakota people for subsistence, the Indians grew more dependent on their Great White Father in Washington for basic survival. The missionaries were trying to teach them the white settler way of life, with limited success. And when the U.S. Government's tardiness in paying the Dakota Indians the annuities due under those treaties and a variety of other factors precipitated Dakota raids on white settlements along the Minnesota River, men who had volunteered to go South to fight the Confederates were diverted home to bring peace back to the countryside. After the war, availability of land brought veterans and other settlers to Minnesota and points further west.

Today, with ever-increasing information available through the internet, the search for Civil War era ancestors is easier than ever before. This guide will provide a road map to that journey in Minnesota, whether your ancestor or not served in a Minnesota regiment.

Acknowledgements

I've always been interested in Minnesota history, an avocation which seems to have taken over many other facets of my life. First was the history of my family, with German ancestors on my maternal side who lived in Henderson at the time of the Dakota Conflict. Great-great-grandfather Anton Röst, a butcher, contracted with the U.S. Government to sell beef to the Dakota Indians, and Rosina, his wife, ran a hotel in Henderson. Rosina's obituary mentions an Indian who came to their doorstep, asking them to save his life. He had pulled Anton and his sled from the Minnesota River on one of his delivery runs. History became personal!

Then Alan Woolworth, Research Fellow Emeritus of the Minnesota Historical Society, took me under his wing, and began sharing with me the wealth of materials on the Dakota Conflict and Minnesota's involvement in the Civil War. He taught me about the different tribes of Dakota: the Mdewakaton, Wapekute, and so on, and then guided me through the preparation of my book on the Spirit Lake Massacre, *Legends, Letters, and Lies*. I knew that somehow his teaching would need to be passed on to other genealogists.

My readers, Steve Osman from Fort Snelling, and Kathy Otto and Hamp Smith from the Minnesota Historical Society Library, offered great comments to ensure that the book would be helpful to those seeking to research in their facilities. Curt Dahlin took time from his own manuscript on the Dakota Conflict to review this one. My friend and editor, Antona Richardson, continues to keep me focused and grounded. She patiently reads what I write, suggesting improvements, helping me prune what is unnecessary and explaining why something that may be clear to me may not be clear to others.

I thank them all. Without each of them, this book would not exist.

– Mary Hawker Bakeman

Beginning a Family History Search

After hearing family stories, the first hint that an ancestor really served in the Civil War is often a marker in the cemetery, with some cryptic information and perhaps a Grand Army of the Republic (GAR) emblem. For me, it was a brief mention in an obituary that a Dakota Indian had saved my great-great-grandfather's life and asked for protection during the Dakota Conflict. Curiosity about whether that was true transformed my general interest in Minnesota history into a very personal search for answers. That find began a trail well-marked with a smorgasbord of resources, from census and naturalization records, personal letters and diaries to descriptions of camp life and boredom, and marches through the countryside and cities destroyed by battle. Library shelves hold treasures detailing everyday life. Newspapers of the day provide clues to the political atmosphere and attitudes toward war. Photography was in its infancy, but images of soldiers and officers do exist, along with maps of battlefields with descriptions by those who fought there. Where to start is the question. This guide will help.

The topic of Dakota Indian and Mètis (mixed blood) genealogy is far too complex to be covered adequately in a book about researching Civil War military. The records required for success differ greatly. In addition, the Dakota conflict was not universally approved among the Dakota Indians living in Minnesota. Some were eager to join the fight; others assisted in rescuing white settlers. If you find your ancestor among those involved in the Dakota conflict in any way, your reading should include sources which explain both sides of the conflict.

The Historical Setting

Family stories can be a mixture of facts, embellishments and misunderstandings. Still, they remain a personal, family connection to events of the past. While no one else may have written your family history, with some research, you can!

An understanding of history can provide context to answer questions that arise when researching a family. For example, why did my German (or Swedish or Irish) ancestors choose to settle in Minnesota in the 1850s? How did they decide what land to buy? What did they bring with them? Who traveled with them? What were their lives like? Where can I find their birth, marriage and death dates and the official records of those events? Explanations are often found in the historical context.

In a short time, a researcher is likely to find names spelled in a variety of ways in different records, errors in published records and problems with indexes. Don't give up! Putting together the pieces of a family puzzle can be very rewarding, and an addictive hobby. The most successful researchers continually evaluate each new piece as to where it can connect to information they already have, and where it can lead to new possibilities.

Researchers are strongly encouraged to develop and document basic details about the entire family, including names, birthdates and the family's migration pattern.

Sample – Anton/Rosina (Mueller) Röst family Timeline	
23 Dec 1853	marriage, Herbertingen, Wurtemburg, Germany
2 May 1854	arrival in New York on the *Meldon* (obit)
3 July 1854	arrival in St. Paul, take claim outside Stillwater
24 Dec 1854	daughter Mary born in Lake Elmo, Washington Co., Minn.
6 Feb 1856	son Charles born in Henderson, Sibley Co., Minn.
4 May 1857	son John born
Oct 1858	**census** taken for Minn. Territory to become a state; family in Henderson
28 Oct 1858	daughter Louisa born
June 1860	**Federal census**, family living in Henderson
12 Oct 1860	daughter Rosala baptized in Jessenland, Sibley Co.
July 1862	daughter Clara baptized in Jessenland
17 Nov 1864	twin daughters Pauline and Phillipina baptized in Jessenland
June 1865	**state census**; family in Henderson
Nov 1865	family moves to St. Peter, Nicollet Co., Minn.
11 Jul 1867	son Anton Joseph born in St. Peter
June 1870	**Federal census**, family living in St. Peter

This partial timetable illustrates the diversity of records which can be used to follow a family's migration. This family participated in the Dakota Conflict in Henderson, supplying goods to the military. Both Anton and Rosina died in St. Peter.

Geography plays an important role in identifying where records can be found, as well as in determining which "John Anderson" is the right one! Obituaries from the local newspapers, vital statistic records from the township or county of residence, naturalization papers, Federal and Minnesota censuses, city, county and other local histories, gravestone inscriptions, etc., can assist in this process.

The techniques for genealogical research remain constant, while the specific resources change. This guide describes special resources for Minnesota, and more specifically resources for the Civil War era. The place to begin each step of your search is listed first.

There are many excellent references on techniques and resources for family history, particularly in the United States, including the following:

- Croom, Emily Anne, *The Genealogist's Companion & Sourcebook (2nd revision)*, Cincinnati, Ohio: Betterway Books, 2003. Includes instructions for where to start your research, documenting the facts gathered, evaluating them, developing a research plan, citing references and sharing your research with others, as well as bibliographical references and a good index.

- Szucs, Loretto Dennis and Luebking, Sandra Hargreaves, editors, *The Source: A Guidebook of American Genealogy (revised edition)*, Salt Lake City, Utah: Ancestry, 1997. Includes thorough descriptions of the variety of records kept in the United States that can be used for genealogical research, with bibliographical references and index.

- <www.familysearch.org>, the on-line website sponsored by the Church of Jesus Christ of the Latter-day Saints (Mormon), provides instructional materials as well as an on-line catalog for the Family History Libraries. Microfilms of original records from around the world have been made available to all family historians through the work of that church.

Other books can help you find resources for New England, Germany, Scandinavia, Ireland, etc. As you gain expertise, you will find these resources and others helpful in suggesting new avenues and clues in your further research. Everyone hits a 'brick wall' eventually: they will help you go around it.

Federal Census Records

After gathering as much information as possible from family members, the Federal census is a good next step. The United States began compiling census statistics in **1790** as a way of determining military strength following the American Revolution and representation in Congress. Early censuses reported the name of the head of household with the number of 'others' in the household.

As settlers moved west, other questions were added to the enumeration of the population, often on separate sheets, called schedules. The listing of families was made on a population schedule, and the other questions were non-population schedules. For example, the **1850-1880** censuses included an agricultural schedule with questions about the amount of land cleared, livestock, crops, etc., a social statistic schedule, with information about newspapers, crime, churches, schools, etc., and a mortality schedule, with information about deaths occurring in the prior twelve months. The **1890** census included a separate schedule for veterans. All these schedules provide useful information to the family historian.

The taking of a federal census every ten years continues today, with different questions each time. The schedules are not made available for research by the public until after 72 years to protect the privacy of those who are listed on it.

The census was taken by enumerators in carefully described geographic areas, such as townships, villages, precincts and wards within major cities. If you know where your ancestor lived, it is relatively simple to review the listing for that area to find them. City directories (which list addresses and occupations) can help locate residents in metropolitan areas. The Minnesota Historical Society Library

A page of a population schedule from 1860 Federal census.

holds a collection of city directories for Minnesota cities that can help locate a family if an index is not available. Public libraries in Duluth, St. Paul, Minneapolis and other cities hold directories for their cities.

In **1850**, the first every-name census was taken which included the place (usually state or country) of birth for each person. With the influx of Europeans to the United States, that practice assists the researcher in determining when the immigrant ancestor arrived and where to search for naturalization, marriage and birth records.

Population schedules beginning in **1850** list the names of all persons living in particular families, with varying other pieces of information. By compiling the locations given for each member of the family from the census, a rough migration history can be developed. Since the keeping of birth, marriage and death records is typically in the hands of local government, that history can assist in locating other family information.

The official enumeration day of the **1860** census was 1 June 1860. All questions asked were supposed to refer to that date. Included in the census were the following categories: name; age as of the census day; sex; color; birthplace; occupation of persons over age fifteen; value of real estate; whether married within the previous year; whether deaf, dumb, blind, insane, a pauper, or a convict; whether able to read or speak English; and whether the person attended school within the previous year. No relationships were shown between members of a household.

At least two published indexes exist for the 1860 Minnesota census. The first, compiled by Accelerated Indexing from the National Archives microfilm of the federal copy of the population schedules, is available in book form in many libraries. The second was completed by the Minnesota Works Progress Administration (WPA) in the 1930s from the state copy of the population schedules. It is available on microfilm at the Minnesota Historical Society Library, or can be purchased or obtained through interlibrary loan. A third by <Ancestry.com>[1] is linked to images of the census pages themselves on-line. This index allows searches of all states simultaneously, a wonderful feature if you aren't sure where the ancestor lived, and a frustration if your ancestor has a common name.

Always look beyond the index at the actual entry/ies on the original records to find other pieces of information that may be relevant to your search. And because of the many opportunities for error in the development of any index, not finding someone on the index does not mean that he or she isn't listed on the

---

[1] <Ancestry.com> is a subscription service available on the internet. Some libraries in Minnesota offer the library version of the service free to their patrons.

Sample of the 1890 Veterans schedule. The form was divided into two sections, with the service record of the veteran in the top section, and pension information in the bottom section.

schedule itself. The indexer may have skipped that line, misread the handwriting, mis-keyed the index entry, or combined it with another entry. Knowing the specific location where a person lived at the time the census was taken allows a researcher to review the population schedules themselves in a convenient fashion.

Special Schedules of the Eleventh Census (1890) Enumerating Union Veterans and Widows of Union Veterans of the Civil War. Though the 1890 population schedules were lost to fire in the 1920s, the veterans schedule from that census exists. Those to be listed on the schedule were "those who had served in the Army, Navy, or Marine Corps of the United States in the war of the rebellion, and who are survivors at the time of said inquiry, and the widows of soldiers, sailors, or marines."

Data collected includes the name of surviving veteran or widow; rank; company; regiment or vessel; date of enlistment; date of discharge; length of service; post office address; disability incurred; and remarks. The key to researching the veteran's military records is the name of the regiment or vessel. The National Archives has microfilmed these schedules as M123, 118 rolls, with Minnesota on rolls 22-25. The Minnesota Historical Society Library holds these films as well, or you can request them at your local Family History Library or public library.

Roll 22. Blue Earth, Brown, Cottonwood, Dodge, Faribault, Fillmore, Freeborn, Houston, Jackson, Lac qui Parle, Lincoln, Lyon, Martin, Mower, Murray, Nicollet, Nobles, Olmsted, Pipestone, Redwood, Rock, Steele, Waseca, Watonwan, Winona, and Yellow Medicine counties, and certain federal, state, local, and private institutions.

Roll 23. Big Stone, Carver, Chippewa, Dakota, Goodhue, Hennepin, Kandiyohi, Le Sueur, McLeod, Meeker, Renville, Rice, Scott, Sibley, Swift, Wabasha, and Wright counties

Roll 24. Aitkin, Anoka, Benton, Carlton, Cass, Chisago, Cook, Crow Wing, Isanti, Itasca, Kanabec, Lake, Mille Lacs, Morrison, Pine, Ramsey, St. Louis, Sherburne, and Washington counties

Roll 25. Becker, Beltrami, Clay, Douglas, Grant, Hubbard, Kittson, Marshall, Norman, Otter Tail, Polk, Pope, Stearns, Stevens, Todd, Traverse, Wadena, and Wilkin counties

The *1890 Minnesota Census Index of Civil War Veterans or Their Widows*, compiled by Bryan Lee Dilts (Salt Lake City: Index. Pub., 1985), is a published alphabetic index by surname. Researchers should always try to view the original document to get the whole story, as indexes seldom include all the available information!

Both the 1910 and the 1930 federal census include questions which can confirm military service and help differentiate between people with the same name.

Federal Census Availability

The federal census from 1790 through 1930 is readily available for family history research. Microfilm copies produced by the National Archives are available at its

Sample of the 1895 Minnesota census, showing the notation for a veteran of the Civil War.

regional branches, at many libraries, or can be obtained by interlibrary loan at your local public library or Family History Library. The Minnesota Historical Society (MHS) holds copies of all Minnesota schedules, as well as some from other states, and many published indexes. In addition, it holds those covering the area before 1849 when Minnesota became a Territory. Wilson Library at the University of Minnesota holds the entire 1870 and 1920 Federal census, as well as the schedules for Minnesota from 1850-1920 in its periodicals collection. A small scattering of other Federal censuses is held in the Wilson Library Annex.

Large genealogical libraries, such as the Allen County Public Library in Fort Wayne, Indiana, and the Wisconsin State Historical Society Library in Madison, Wisconsin, hold complete sets of the federal censuses and finding aids. Smaller libraries are most likely to hold only those portions of the census which cover their local geographic area.

<Ancestry.com>, a subscription service on the internet, offers on-line access to Federal census population schedules and some indexes for them. This service has been purchased by some public libraries for use by their patrons, and is also available for purchase by individuals.

Kathleen W. Hinckley's book, *Your Guide to the Federal Census* [Cincinnati, Ohio: Betterway Books, 2002], contains a good overview of the different schedules used at different times for the Federal census, information on availability of finding aids, extraction forms, etc. The 1930 census is included in Hinckley's guide.

Minnesota State Census

The federal census is supplemented by the Minnesota state census, with every-name population schedules from 1865-1905. They are only partially indexed, and include more limited data than the federal schedules, but are still valuable. The 1865, 1885 and 1905 censuses include a question about military service, for example, and the 1895 census asks how long has the person lived in Minnesota, and how long has that person resided in the same specific area. This information is invaluable in helping develop the family's migration timeline, needed for vital records research.

The Minnesota state census was published on microfilm by the Minnesota Historical Society, and can be obtained through interlibrary loan at your local public library. The *Minnesota State Census Guide* published by Park Genealogical Books in 2001 lists the counties reporting for each of the five Minnesota censuses between 1865-1905, information on which microfilm to use for each census, and extraction forms. It can be used to determine which reel to order for particular townships and counties.

Cemetery Research

A visit to the cemetery where your family is buried can provide clues for additional research. Inscriptions on gravestones may include military service information. Larger cemeteries may have a section called "The Soldiers' Rest" where veterans are buried. In addition, many local newspapers include listings of local boys who served in the military in their coverage of Decoration Day (now Memorial Day). Some compilations have been published as separate booklets. The National Parks Service, through the Soldiers & Sailors System [see page 25], will eventually include an index to those buried in national cemeteries and Medal of Honor recipients. Those buried in local cemeteries in Minnesota are typically survivors of the war or those who died in Minnesota.

Gravestone for Franz Massopust family, victims of the Dakota Conflict, in Brown County. [Photo courtesy of Bob Paulson.]

However, white settlers killed during the Dakota Conflict were not always identified, but buried quickly near where they fell. Communities along the Minnesota River often placed monuments in the memory of all from the area who died. Knowing the geographical location where your family lived can help identify the right cemetery or monument.

For those searching for cemeteries in Minnesota, the best reference is Wiley Pope and Sarah Fee's book entitled *Minnesota Cemetery Locations* (second edition), [St. Paul: Minnesota Family Trees, 1998]. This valuable reference provides a compilation of cemetery locations from maps, county histories, WPA records, and other sources, including private, abandoned and current cemeteries. The legal description of the cemetery land with Township, Range and Section numbers allows them to be located on current maps whether or not the names have changed.

The Minnesota GenWeb

The Minnesota GenWeb is an on-line service maintained by volunteers to help family researchers find resources. The main state page can be found at <http://www.rootsweb.com/~mngenweb/>, from which the pages that refer to the specific county or topic that is of interest can be accessed.

Shortcuts

In brief, there aren't any! Only the basics were covered here. The more facts you gather about an entire family, the easier your future research will be. Family stories which have been passed from generation to generation can be verified by checking other records. Sometimes you will find conflicting information, such as different spellings of the surname, or instances in which a relative used a middle name or initials. All can be helpful in locating other records for family members. **Birth** records provide a new generation to search, and **death** records sometimes do as well. Marriage records can help identify the family religion, leading to church records, often more complete than governmental records.

Probate records list the names and locations for all heirs, and in combination with wills, may explain why some of the family stayed put after the patriarch's death while others moved. In addition, lists showing the distribution of property or the assignment of guardians for minor children contribute to the identification of new surnames for daughters or widows who remarry.

Land records report what happened to the family farm or business. For farmers, a landownership map often illustrates the nearest community, school and church, along with the names of neighbors. How the land was subdivided over time can provide clues on family relationships.

For immigrants, **naturalization** records (the act of becoming a U.S. citizen) or ship passenger lists can help identify the ancestral village. Minnesota District Court naturalization records are available on microfilm through the Minnesota Historical Society; an index to them is available through the Iron Range Research Center at <http://www.ironrangeresearchcenter.org>. The Center will also provide copies for a fee. Federal Court naturalization records from Minnesota are held by the regional branches of the National Archives, with some in Kansas City and some in Chicago. S description of which records are in each branch can be found on-line at
<http://www.parkbooks.com/Html/res_nat9.html>.

Every census, Federal and State, can add something new to your research. For example, children named on the 1870 Federal census but who do not appear on the 1875 State census may have married, moved in with a relative or died. Gather all the information you can – it will open new doors for you.

Did the family photos or Bible or cache of letters written from the battlefields go with that other branch of the family instead of yours?

Minnesota Research Bookshelf

- Bakeman, Mary Hawker, *Minnesota State Census Guide*, Roseville, Minnesota: Park Genealogical Books, 2001. Includes maps of the counties at the time of each census and an extraction form for each of the state census years from 1865-1905, and a listing of which townships and villages are on each reel of microfilm.

- —, *Genealogist's Guide to Minnesota Vital Records: Vol. 1: Marriages and Divorces*. Roseville, Minnesota: Park Genealogical Books, 2002. Laws and availability by county of the records, whether microfilmed, dates covered, and location.

- —, *Genealogist's Guide to Minnesota Vital Records: Vol. 2: Births and Deaths*, Roseville, Minnesota: Park Genealogical Books, 2004. Laws affecting registration, specific dates for records at the village, township, county and state levels of government, and availability on microfilm or location.

- —, *Minnesota Land Owner Maps and Directories*, Roseville, Minnesota: Park Genealogical Books, 1994. Extensive annotated bibliography of maps dating from the mid-1960s to the present day, including wall maps, atlases, reprints, micofiche and film, and indexes, plus rural resident directories.

- Pope, Wiley and Fee, Sarah *Minnesota Cemetery Locations* (second edition), St. Paul: Minnesota Family Trees, 1998. Compendium of sites from geographic survey, plat and other maps, printed references, etc.

- Stuart-Warren, Paula, *Minnesota Genealogical Reference Guide*, St. Paul: Stuart-Warren Consulting, 2005 (7th edition). Overview relating to Minnesota genealogical research, including sources, websites, searching on location, etc.

The Minnesota Historical Society is publishing a series of books on various ethnic groups in Minnesota, *Germans in Minnesota, Poles in Minnesota, Norwegians in Minnesota*, etc. These are helpful in understanding the historical context for the ethnic patterns of settlement within the state.

Park Genealogical Books' free monthly research notes are available on the internet at <http://www.parkbooks.com/Html/research.html>.

Getting Familiar with Military Terminology

Successful research requires a basic understanding of the specialized terms used in the subject under review. This chapter includes the basic terms you will need to read rosters and regimental histories for your ancestor, and battle histories for the regiment in which he served, and to connect data from various sources.

Minnesota soldiers served in infantry, cavalry, light artillery, heavy artillery and sharpshooter units organized in the state before being accepted (mustered) into federal service. Other Minnesotans served in organizations of other states, especially Wisconsin, and in various federal units including the United States Colored Troops and the United States Navy.

Some Minnesota soldiers were commissioned as officers into newly formed units, and slightly disabled soldiers could join special federal organizations like the Veteran Reserve Corps, two companies of which served at Fort Snelling. Most Minnesota Civil War soldiers were volunteers. Early in the war, a man could enlist for three months. It soon became apparent that the enlistment terms needed to be extended, and most of the soldiers volunteered for three years. Although some three thousand Minnesota residents were drafted into service near the end of the war, only ten percent of those actually ever reported for duty.

The basic building block of military units was the **company**, typically numbering at organization from around 100 to 150 men. Soldiers enlisted by signing their name on a roll and were examined by a doctor; if accepted they were officially mustered into service when their company or its regiment was filled and accepted as part of their state's allotted quota of troops.

Men in companies often came from the same geographic area, and sometimes elected their own officers. The man who recruited them was often initially in command, either by election or appointment, though later promotions were made strictly by seniority. Companies were commanded by commissioned officers–a captain assisted by two or more lieutenants. The captain also appointed non-commissioned officers including a first (or orderly) sergeant who was assisted by three other sergeants and eight corporals. Between 64 and 82 privates filled the ranks. Cavalry and light artillery companies (or batteries) had slightly different numbers and structure. Infantry companies were designated from A to K, excluding J, and cavalry companies from A to M, excluding J.

A partial listing of Company A, Second Minnesota Volunteer Infantry, from the *Adjutant General's Report of 1866*. Note the proximity of the residences.

A partial listing of Company A, Second Minnesota Volunteer Infantry, from *Minnesota in the Civil and Indian Wars, Vol. 1*, published in 1891. The rosters in this source do not include either birth or residence information. Note that some names appear in one listing but not in the other.

Minnesota officers above the company level were usually appointed or commissioned by the governor. Minnesota troops received clothing, arms and some drill instruction at Fort Snelling as they organized and were mustered into federal service. Many went on to serve a sort of apprenticeship, in rotation, at the state's Forts Ridgely, Ripley and Abercrombie. At the end of their three-year enlistment the survivors were mustered out, again usually with their unit.

Companies rarely served alone, but were organized into regiments or (somewhat smaller) battalions. Only Minnesota's three light artillery batteries and two companies of sharpshooters were mustered individually but then assigned to larger units after they left the state. Infantry **regiments** were composed of ten companies or around one thousand men, and heavy artillery and cavalry regiments of twelve companies. Regiments were commanded by a colonel assisted by a lieutenant colonel and one or two majors, plus field and staff officers including surgeons, quartermaster and commissary officers.

Regiments, batteries and battalions from Minnesota were placed into larger units when they reached the front. A **brigade** was usually composed of four regiments, under the command of a brigadier general and either named for him or designated First, Second, Third Brigade and so forth. The regiments often came from different states and could be shifted from one brigade to another as needed; it was not unusual for a regiment to serve as part of several brigades dur-

Abbreviations commonly used by the War Department

A.Q.M.	Assistant Quartermaster of Volunteers	Indep.	Independent
		Inf.	Infantry
A.A.G	Assistant Adjutant General of Volunteers	L. Art.	Light Artillery
		Mech.	Mechanic
A.C.S.	Assistant Commissary of Subsistence	Mil.	Militia
		Mtd.	Mounted
Adj't.	Regimental Adjutant	Q.M.	Quartermaster
Art.	Artillery	Q.M.D.	Quartermaster Department
Bn.	Battalion	Regt.	Regiment
Bvt.	Brevet	R.Q.M.	Regimental Quartermaster
Brig.	Brigade	R.C.S.	Regimental Commissary of Subsistence
Btry.	Battery		
Cav.	Cavalry	Squad.	Squadron
Engs.	Engineers	SS	Sharp Shooters
Enroll.	Enrolled	Unassign.	Unassigned
F & S	Field and Staff	Unatt.	Unattached
H. Art.	Heavy Artillery	U.S.A.	U.S. Regular Army
H.G.	Home Guard	Vet.	Veterans
Hosp.	Hospital	V.R.C.	Veterans Reserve Corps
IC	Invalid Corps	Vols.	Volunteers
Ind. Terr	Indian Territory	VV	Veteran Volunteers

ing its career. Artillery batteries and cavalry troops were sometimes attached to brigades.

A **division** was made up of from two to five brigades, and was commanded by brigadier or major general and typically known by the name of its commander. **Corps** were the next larger organizations, and composed of several divisions plus artillery and cavalry. Initially known by its commanding major general's name, corps were later numbered and each given a distinctive insignia for its men to wear. The largest organization, the **army**, had two or more corps plus unattached units of artillery and cavalry. The Union armies were known by the names of rivers (the Army of the Potomac, the Army of the Cumberland). Confederate armies were named after their states.

The Adjutant General was the top state-appointed military officer in Minnesota, as required for each state by an act of Congress dated May 8, 1792. In 1858, the new state of Minnesota legally created this office, filled by gubernatorial appointment, to serve a seven-year term. The Adjutant General commanded the state militia, and assisted in turning newly-raised state forces over to federal authority.

General John Sanborn, later governor, was Adjutant General during the critical year of 1861 and managed the raising, equipping and deployment of the state's first several regiments. He resigned to assume field command of the Fourth Minnesota Volunteer Infantry. He was born in New Hampshire in 1826, arrived in Minnesota Territory in 1854 and died in St. Paul fifty years later, achieving a notable career in both the military and public service.

Oscar Malmros next served as Adjutant General of Minnesota. The records of his office document the creation and service of Minnesota's military during the remainder of the Civil War. He prepared annual reports to the governor and the legislature on topics such as recruiting, equipment, battles, and losses. His report for 1866 lists the 23,000+ soldiers recruited in Minnesota for the Civil War. Malmros was born in Germany in 1826, and died in Rouen, France on 18 August 1909. He came to the United States when he was twenty-six years old, and settled in St. Paul in 1853. Following the Civil War, he served as U.S. Consul in Turkey, and later as consul in Spain and other countries.

Most Minnesota soldiers served in **infantry** units, such as the Fifth Regiment Minnesota Volunteer Infantry. These men marched by foot and fought with muskets or rifle muskets tipped with a bayonet. Minnesota fielded a total of eleven infantry regiments and one smaller battalion between 1861 and 1865. Some fought in the Dakota Conflict and most saw some frontier duty before heading south or east to fight the Confederacy. Two companies of sharpshooters, armed with breech-loading rifles, were posted to the eastern theater of the war.

Cavalry units mounted on horseback were needed to defend the frontier after the Dakota Conflict of 1862. Brackett's Battalion of Minnesota Cavalry was the first, which initially did duty in the south (1861-1863) as part of an Iowa regiment. The First Regiment of Minnesota Mounted Rangers, a twelve-company regiment that served one year of frontier defense duty, was followed in late 1863 by the Second Regiment Minnesota Cavalry and the smaller Hatch's Battalion. Neither of the latter two units were sent south, but remained on duty into the summer of 1866, a full year after most veterans had returned to civilian life.

Other Minnesotans manned the cannons of the state's three **light artillery** batteries. The first two batteries fought in the south and the third joined them after campaigning against Dakota Indians on the 1863 Sibley Expedition and the 1864 Sully Expedition. Each battery was armed with six cannons, each attached to a limber (cart) carrying an ammunition chest and pulled by six horses. Each cannon also had a caisson carrying two more ammunition chests and also pulled by six horses. Commanded by a captain, artillery batteries were served by around 150 men and needed nearly as many horses. Light artillery was always supported by, and used in support of, other troops. It was highly mobile, and its men acquired considerable skill as the war progressed.

The First Regiment Minnesota **Heavy Artillery** was raised in the fall of 1864 and assigned to man forts in the middle south and guard transportation routes. Known also as foot artillery or siege artillery, these soldiers were trained to operate larger cannons but were usually armed and used as infantry. Because of their shorter service and no combat action, most Minnesotans in this unit were mustered out with their companies. The last surviving Civil War soldier on either north or south, Albert Woolson of Duluth, served with this regiment.

All able bodied military-age men were considered part of the Minnesota militia, organized into units which existed on paper only, until the Dakota Conflict of 1862, when dozens of local militia or home guards units were organized and did duty on a temporary basis protecting their communities and farms along the Minnesota River. They built fortifications to protect the refugees, staffed hospitals for the wounded, joined together to scout the countryside for supplies and food, and provided relief. They were first armed with their own weapons until the state distributed thousands of old European muskets and other arms in 1863.

A history of each Minnesota unit with a roster of those who served was published in *Minnesota in the Civil and Indian Wars* (St. Paul: Minnesota Board of Commissions on Publication of History of Minnesota in Civil and Indian Wars, 1890-1893 [reprint available in 2005]. They are first-person accounts, recounting the formation of the unit, the battles it fought, remarkable events, and its mustering out. They are basic reading for anyone researching a soldier in a Minnesota regiment or as a citizen soldier during the Dakota Conflict. These histories have been reprinted by Park Genealogical Books as separate booklets for each infantry regiment, the cavalry units, the artillery units, the sharpshooters, and those citizen soldiers who served during the Dakota Conflict.

More information on the effects of the Dakota Conflict on non-military personnel and the home guard can be found in the chapter 'Civilians at Home' [see page 51]. Military records are the same for soldiers who served on the frontier or in the south in the U.S. forces in the 1861-1865 time frame.

Major Repositories of Civil War Information

Researching a family requires putting together pieces from many different sources. The same is true for Civil War research, whether you are primarily interested in discovering where your ancestor fought, or what kind of disability he suffered, or how he felt about his military service. The repositories listed here are the primary sources of information. Some sources provide information on the internet, on microfilm or in published form. But they also hold many unpublished materials that might be relevant to your search. These repositories are treasure stores of memorabilia as well as text materials and are worthwhile visiting at some point during your research.

The National Archives (NARA)
700 Pennsylvania Avenue NW
Washington, DC 20408-0001
on-line at <http://www.archives.gov>

Located in Washington, D.C., the National Archives is the nation's attic, preserving federal documents and making them available to researchers. Among the items of specific interest for Minnesota Civil War researchers are military post returns, reports from the battlefields, officer recruiting for service in the U.S. Colored Troops, reports from the Indian agencies, Lincoln's review of the Dakota Indian trials and decision on commuting sentences, pensions for those who served and their survivors, payment of military and depredation claims, and more.

The broad interest in the Civil War has resulted in the microfilming of many federal records, making them available for use in many locations. Instead of one original set of records available in a single location, all or part of a microfilm set can be purchased by other repositories or individuals, or can be obtained through interlibrary loan at local public libraries. Throughout this guide, an attempt has been made to identify other Minnesota repositories which hold key federal microfilm sets.

- *Regional Facilities:* Some National Archives and Records Administration (NARA) regional facilities have selected microfilmed Civil War compiled military service records and other microfilmed military records; call to verify their availability. All have complete sets of the Federal census microfilm. A list of the Regional Facilities can be found at <http://www.archives.gov/locations/regional-archives.html>.

- *URL genealogy research:* Information about availability of records, how to use them for family history, access to its catalogs, and more is available through the National Archives genealogy pages at <http://www.archives.gov/genealogy/>

Special National Archives Finding Aids

- Eals, Ann Bruner and Kvasnicka, Robert M. *Guide to Genealogical Research in the National Archives of the United States (third edition)*, Washington, D.C.: National Archives and Records Administration, 2000

- Munden, Kenneth W., and Henry Putney Beers. *The Union: A Guide to Federal Archives Relating to the Civil War.* National Archives and Records Administration. 1962. Reprint, 1986. [There is a similar volume for the Confederacy.]

- *A Guide to Civil War Maps in the National Archives.* National Archives and Records Administration. 1964. Reprint, 1986.

- *Military Service Records: A Select Catalog of National Archives Microfilm Publications.* Washington, DC: National Archives and Records Administration, 1985. Available online at <http://www.archives.gov/publications/microfilm-catalogs/military-service-records/index.html>.

Civil War Soldiers &Sailors System (CWSS)
<http://www.itd.nps.gov/cwss/>
A National Park Service (NPS) program

The Civil War Soldiers & Sailors System is a computerized database containing basic facts about 6.3 million servicemen who served on both sides during the Civil War and is fully searchable, by personal name, unit or state. The facts provide access to many millions of documents about Union and Confederate Civil War soldiers which are maintained by the National Archives. In addition, most national parks include a national cemetery, and this site will eventually include burial information as well.

Other information includes: histories of regiments in both the Union and Confederate Armies, links to descriptions of 384 significant battles of the war, and other historical information. Additional information about soldiers, sailors, regiments, and battles, as well as prisoner-of-war records and cemetery records, will be added over time.

Library of Congress (LOC)

<http://www.loc.gov/>
101 Independence Avenue SE
Washington, D.C. 20540

The Library of Congress offers many resources to the researcher, through its many specialized collections. Some can be accessed on-line, some can be obtained through local libraries on interlibrary loan, others must be viewed at its facility in Washington, D.C.

- The *National Union Catalog for Manuscript Collections (NUCMC)* includes unpublished manuscripts, diaries, letters, and other materials from a variety of sources which offer an intimate glimpse of the times, battles or life at home. Your ancestor may not have personally written any of these, but may still be mentioned in them. The catalog can be searched on-line, but you'll have to travel to the repository where they are located to use the manuscripts. The URL is <http://lcweb.loc.gov/coll/numc/numc.html>

- The *American Memory Collections* at the Library of Congress feature maps, photographs by Matthew Brady and other photographers, ephemera, reports, and other materials which can round out your family's Civil War story. Their searchable site can be found at <http://memory.loc.gov/ammem/index.html>

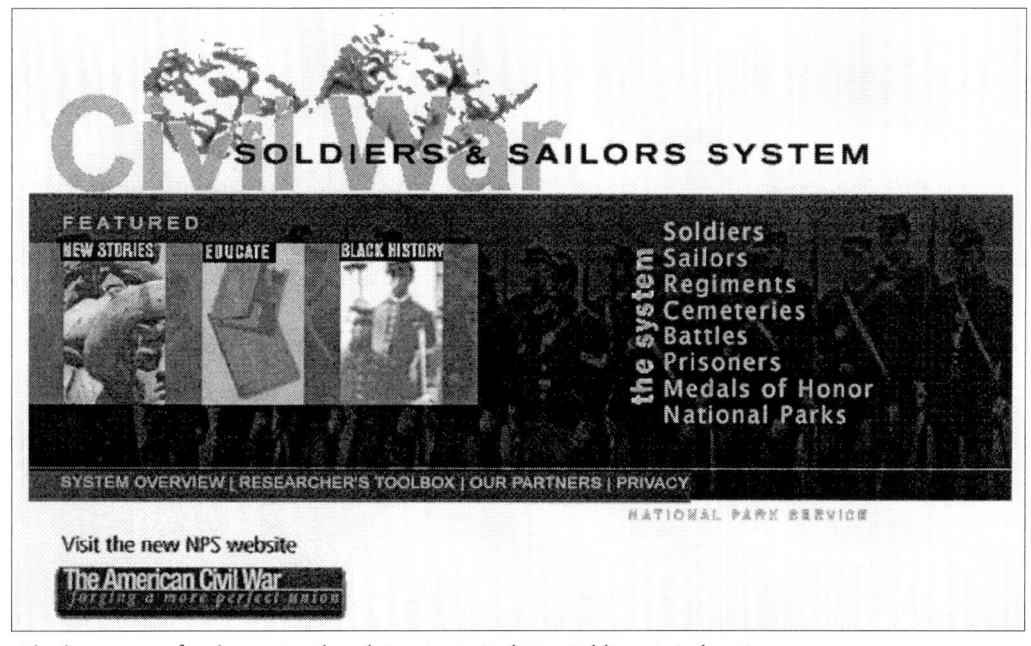

The home page for the National Park Service's Civil War Soldiers & Sailors System.

The Minnesota History Center
Minnesota Historical Society (MHS)
345 Kellogg Boulevard West
St. Paul, Minnesota 55102
Website: <http://www.mnhs.org/>

Established as one of the first acts of the Minnesota Territorial Legislature in 1849, MHS serves as the state historical society and the state archives. As the State Historical Society, it collects materials from many sources that illuminate/represent pieces of Minnesota's history, such as artifacts, photos, visual and audio materials, Civil War uniforms, flags, etc.; it also collects newspapers, books and manuscripts from businesses and individuals about Minnesota; as the state archives, it is the official repository for records at all levels of government, from local units such as watershed and school districts, to regional and statewide organizations such as the Adjutant General, the Minnesota Grand Army of the Republic (GAR), the Minnesota Supreme Court and the Minnesota Department of Health. Archives records are arranged by branch of government or state agency and are accessed through the archives inventory notebooks found in the Weyerhaeuser Reference Room at the MHS. These records are also listed in the on-line catalog, accessible through the Society's web page. Searches can be as general as "Dakota Conflict" and "Civil War Minnesota" or as specific as an individual's name or unit designation.

Minnesota has preserved many resources for researchers. The 1891 *Minnesota in the Civil and Indian Wars*, a two-volume set with regimental histories and rosters in one volume and official correspondence and records in the other, provides a fundamental resource for researchers. Minnesota soldiers and others lobbied for monuments on the battlefields, and raised funds for their erection. Four large oil paintings commemorating turning points in the war and the Minnesota troops's participation in it hang in the Governor's Reception Room at the State Capitol.

Historic sites along the Minnesota River operated along the Minnesota River commemorate the Dakota conflict, including Fort Ridgely, the Lower Sioux Agency and others. They are worth a visit! The Minnesota Historical Society collection of manuscripts and eye-witness accounts have been microfilmed as the *Dakota Conflict of 1862 Manuscript Collection*. This microfilm is available through local public libraries on interlibrary loan.

The Society's **website** <http://www.mnhs.org/> includes many resources for family historians, including their on-line catalog, an index to Minnesota deaths and birth records, a geographical reference to Minnesota place names, an index to its journal *Minnesota History*, the graves registration index [see page 38] and more.

The Society's **Civil War card file** in the Library Reading Room lists veterans who lived in Minnesota, whether or not they served in Minnesota regiments. The information includes unit, GAR affiliation, and pension information.

The Society's **visual resources database** includes photographs, postcards, art, and other materials. There are photographs of Civil War soldiers (mostly officers), Fort Snelling, some of the Indians involved in the Dakota Conflict, and much more. Not all images are digitized or included in this database. When you visit, check the card catalog and collections notebooks for more.

Special MHS Finding Aids

- MHS Reference Staff, *A Guide to Family History Resources at the Minnesota Historical Society*, St. Paul: Minnesota Historical Society, 2004.

- Smith, Hampton, *Resources for Civil War History at the Minnesota Historical Society*. St. Paul: Minnesota Historical Society (available on-line at the MHS website), 1998. Though specializing in Minnesota materials, the Society holds an excellent collection of published materials from other states, including rosters for twenty-one other states, including both Union and Confederate forces.

- Osman, Stephen, *Minnesota in the Civil War, 1861-1866: A Bibliography of Published Sources.* St. Paul: Minnesota Historical Society (also at Fort Snelling), unpublished manuscript, various editions.

Minnesota County Historical Societies

see <http://www.mnhs.org/preserve/mho/chsclo.html>
for contact information

The Civil War was a very personal war. Many soldiers wrote letters home and to the local newspapers and many kept diaries. Following the war, those who had enlisted and served together participated together in fraternal organizations such as the Grand Army of the Republic or 'last man clubs,' sharing their experiences. Officers and others wrote regimental histories, spoke at reunions or other gatherings, and joined together in efforts to preserve memories through monuments and books. County histories often included listings of Civil War soldiers. County historical societies ensured that the stories of their residents would endure. They may have a personal account written by one of your ancestors or a photo or other item among their collections.

University of Minnesota - Wilson Library
309 – 19th Avenue South
Minneapolis, Minnesota 55455

This outstanding academic library has many resources available for the family history research. The reference staff has published a guide to the published resources available for Civil War research. This can be found at <http://wilson.lib.umn.edu/reference/civilwar.html>

Public and Academic Libraries

Academic libraries (especially if American history is taught!) and your local public library have many books and other resources about the Civil War. Be sure to ask about obtaining resources they don't have in their own collections through interlibrary loan. Much has been written about the Civil War. The following excellent resources are available in many libraries. You may be able to find your own copy through a used book store, too.

- Morebeck, Nancy Justus, *Locating Union and Confederate Records: A Guide to the Most Commonly Used Civil War Records of the National Archives and Family History Library* is a beginner's guide to Civil War genealogical research.

- Long, Everette B. *Civil War Day by Day: An Almanac, 1861-1865*. Garden City, NY: Doubleday, 1971.

- Catton, Bruce. *The Centennial History of the Civil War*. 3 vols. Garden City, NY: Doubleday, 1961-65.

- Foote, Shelby. *The Civil War*. 3 vols. New York, NY: Random House, 1958-74.

- McPherson, James M., *Battle Cry of Freedom: the Civil War Era*. New York: Oxford University Press, 1988. Includes a bibliography and index.

"Must Reads" - Minnesota Resources

- Carley, Kenneth, *Minnesota in the Civil War: An Illustrated History*, St. Paul, Minnesota: Minnesota Historical Society Press, 2000.

- Carley, Kenneth, *The Dakota War of 1862: Minnesota's Other Civil War*, St. Paul, Minnesota: Minnesota Historical Society Press, 2001.

- Anderson, Gary Clayton and Woolworth, Alan R., *Through Dakota Eyes: Narrative Accounts of the Minnesota Indian War of 1862*, St. Paul, Minnesota: Minnesota Historical Society Press, 1988.

First, Research Your Ancestor

You may already have some idea about your ancestor's service from an inscription on a gravestone, family letters or from your census review. The records describing his service are most likely to be found with those for the unit in which he served. The military organization required regular monthly musters in preparation for paying the troops and other reports to be turned in to the military hierarchy. Reports include who is sick or on special assignment, requests for supplies, etc., and indicate the unit and the name(s) of the officer reporting.

Units are identified by a designation that includes a number for the regiment, the name of the state from which served, the type of service (Infantry, Cavalry, etc.) and the specific company, e.g., Co. F, 6th Minnesota Infantry. This designation is also important in differentiating between soldiers with the same name, and ensuring that you are tracking the 'right' John Schmidt! And as with other family history research, the spelling of a surname can vary from record to record.

Service Records

The basic information about a soldier is available through his service record. The federal government through the Department of War controlled the overall operation of troops during the Civil War, recruited soldiers into the regular U.S. Army and U.S. Navy, and requisitioned troops from the Union states. To fill their quotas, the state Adjutants General recruited men, who were enrolled into state regiments. Those regiments received basic training and equipment, then were mustered into federal service, where they were combined with regiments of U.S. troops and/or troops from other states into brigades, divisions, corps and armies. For this reason, records for individual soldiers and the units in which they served can usually be found at both the federal and state levels. Some soldiers and units from Minnesota fought only during the Dakota Conflict and were not inducted into federal service. The service records for those soldiers will be found only in Minnesota.

Be sure to check across the state borders into Wisconsin and Iowa military records, if you don't find your Minnesota resident in a Minnesota regiment.

Places to Look

The basic references for Minnesota include both those who served in a military organization and in the home guards or local militia during the Dakota conflict.

- The *Index to the 1866 Minnesota Adjutant General's Report* lists soldiers that were recruited within the State of Minnesota, and is based on contemporary reports. It is available in print, CD or from <Ancestry.com>, and provides name, rank, age, nativity, date enrolled, date mustered in, residence, and remarks as well as the unit in which the soldier served. The detail in this index allows the researcher to distinguish between two or more soldiers with the same name.

  The *Annual Report of the Adjutant General of the State of Minnesota for the Year Ending Dec. 1, 1866, and of Military Forces of the State from 1861 - 1866* (St. Paul, 1866, usually shortened to *1866 Minnesota Adjutant General's Report*) itself can be found in some libraries, including the Minnesota Historical Society. (A sample from it is shown on page 18.) The unit information leads to the unit rosters, published regimental histories, eyewitness accounts, and other papers about the service of the individual and the group with whom he served.

  The records of the Minnesota Adjutant General's Office at the Minnesota Historical Society document the activities of and the enlistees in Minnesota's home defense organizations and wartime regiments. There is an extensive set of muster rolls and other registers, plus general correspondence, official communications, reports, supplies accounts, and other records of the regiments and of the military administration.

- *Compiled Rosters of Minnesota Civil War Regiments* include service information on individuals who performed military service during the Civil War. They were compiled twice by the Minnesota Adjutant General's office, first in 1865 and later in 1915. The 1915 compilation is more complete, and also contains registers of Minnesota draftees and substitutes, enrollees in the U.S. Engineers and the U.S. Colored Troops, and militia units which served only in the Dakota Conflict. Entries generally give name, rank, age, nativity, date and place enrolled and mustered, residence, and remarks (usually on service transfer or termination).

- Irene B. Warming's *Minnesotans in the Civil and Indian Wars: An Index to the Rosters in Minnesota in the Civil and Indian Wars, 1861-1865* (St. Paul: Minnesota Historical Society, 1936) provides a page number reference to the rosters (for a sample, see 18) and the published *1866 Minnesota Adjutant General's Report*. The additional detail in the entry for the *Index to the Report* provided above, makes it more easier to distinguish between two or more soldiers with the same name.

- *Index to Compiled Military Service Records (CMSR) of Volunteer Union Soldiers* on National Archives microfilm from Record Group 94, Records of the U.S. Adjutant General's Office. These microfilms are available at all branches of the National Archives, larger genealogical libraries and are searchable on the internet via the NPS Soldiers & Sailors System at <http://www.itd.nps.gov/cwss/>. The Minnesota Historical Society holds the ten reels which list Minnesota volunteers as microfilm #2. This index leads to the full record for the soldier held by the National Archives.

The NPS Soldiers & Sailors System allows an on-line search by personal name, state, unit, and whether Union or Confederate. Note, too, that this system includes service in the U.S. Colored Troops (USCT), segregated regiments of freed slaves with white officers, many of whom had previously served in other regiments. A number of Minnesota residents served as officers in these regiments.

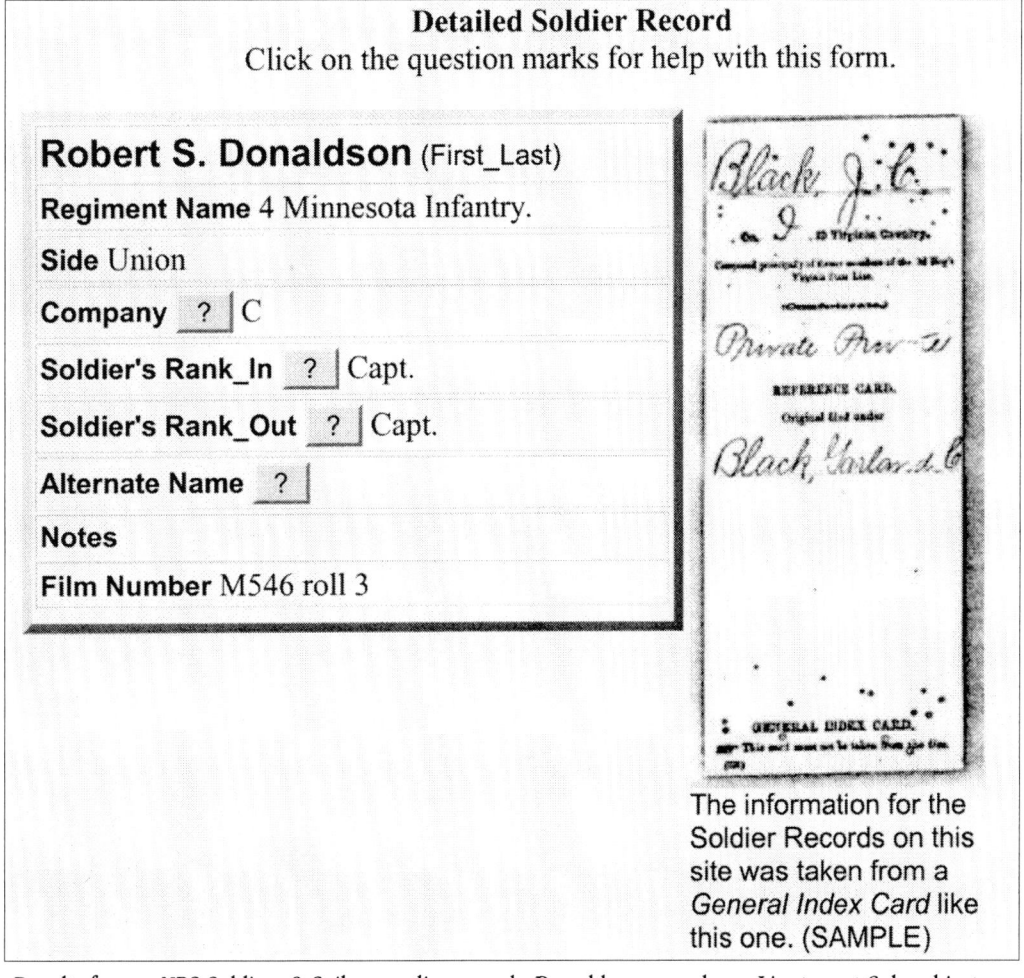

Detailed Soldier Record
Click on the question marks for help with this form.

Robert S. Donaldson (First_Last)
Regiment Name 4 Minnesota Infantry.
Side Union
Company ? C
Soldier's Rank_In ? Capt.
Soldier's Rank_Out ? Capt.
Alternate Name ?
Notes
Film Number M546 roll 3

The information for the Soldier Records on this site was taken from a *General Index Card* like this one. (SAMPLE)

Results from a NPS Soldiers & Sailors on-line search. Donaldson served as a Lieutenant Colonel in two different U.S.C.T. regiments as well as in the 4th Minnesota, and therefore has three entries in the system. The film number reference is to the National Archives microfilm.

The War Department assembled the CMSR to permit rapid and efficient checking of military and medical records in connection with claims for pensions and other veterans' benefits. A CMSR is as complete as the surviving records of an individual soldier or his unit. Information from company muster rolls, regimental returns, descriptive books, hospital rolls, and other records was copied verbatim onto cards. A separate card was prepared each time an individual name appeared on a document. The abstracts were so carefully prepared that it is rarely necessary to consult the original muster rolls and other records from which they were made. The CMSR may contain "personal papers" of various kinds. These may include a copy of the soldier's enlistment paper, papers relating to his capture and release as a prisoner of war, or a statement that he had no personal property with him when he died. Note, however, that the CMSR rarely indicates battles in which a soldier fought; that information must be derived from other sources. Copies of the full CMSR can be purchased from the National Archives either on-line or via mail using Form NATF 86.

- *Registers of Enlistments in the United States Army, 1798-1897* from Record Group 94, Records of the U.S. Adjutant General's Office (National Archives Microcopy 233/Minnesota Historical Society M191—47 reels). The record provides name, age, birthplace, civilian occupation, personal description and enlistment data for those who enlisted into the regular Army. The registers are generally arranged by groups of years, then alphabetically by the first letter of the soldier's surname, then chronologically by date of enlistment. They were compiled from enlistment papers, muster rolls, and other records.

- *List of Pensioners on the Roll: January 1, 1883* (U.S. Senate, 47th Congress, 2nd Session, 1882-1883, S. Doc. 84, Serials 2078-82); pensioners with Minnesota addresses are listed in Serial 2081, pages 531-91 and in the *Minnesota Genealogical Journal 3-6*; reprinted with index by Park Genealogical Books. These lists show pensioners living in each state, arranged by post office in 1883, though they might not have served in regiments from that state.

- **Cemeteries.** There are various resources which can be used to track down burials for those who died during the War and are buried near the battlefields. The *Roll of Honor* [Washington, D.C.: G.P.O., 1865-1871] contains 31 volumes, published as 7 books. The set was compiled by the Quartermaster General's Office and is available at many larger libraries. In addition, all the volumes plus an index and formerly unpublished Roll of Honor burials of more than 200,000 Union soldiers has been published as a CD by Genealogical Publishing Company. The information will be added to the on-line NPS Soldiers & Sailors System in the future.

- **Prisoners of war.** A mention of a Confederate prison such as Andersonville in your ancestor's record opens additional avenues for research. The entire 3rd Minnesota Infantry Regiment was surrendered and sent home, where they provided protection on the frontier. An overloaded steamboat, the *Sultana*, returning prisoners to the north, exploded, killing hundreds. Check library on-line catalogs to find resources to complete that chapter in your ancestor's life. In addition to published materials available through libraries, the National Park Systems website offers glimpses into the conditions experienced by the prisoners. The NPS Soldiers & Sailors System contains data on prisoners of war.

- **Other published listings** exist as well. For example, the United States Christian Commission compiled *Record of the Federal Dead: Buried from Libby, Belle Isle, Danville & Camp Lawton Prisons, and at City Point, and in the Field Before Petersburg and Richmond* from reports of the Commission's agents. It was published in Philadelphia by J.B. Rodgers, printer, in 1866.

- *Civil War Allotment Rolls* and related correspondence from the Minnesota Treasurer's Office and the Minnesota Adjutant General's Office now in the state archives at the MHS include lists of soldiers in the various Minnesota regiments who authorized pay and/or deductions from their pay to be sent to someone other than themselves (e.g., families at home). The lists include name, rank, monthly pay, amount to be sent to assignee, the address of the assignee, the soldier's signature and remarks.

Official Government Reports

Official government reports can make for interesting background reading and of the war effort as it unfolds.

- *Minnesota Governor's Records, 1858-1865.* The following men served in that office during the Civil War: Alexander Ramsey, 1860-1863, Henry A. Swift, 1863-1864 and Stephen Miller, 1864-1865. This series in the state archives at the MHS includes the majority of their official records, including letters received, appointments, accounts and reports.

  There is a wealth of information here on the state's role in the war, including issues such as: the appointment of officers to posts in Minnesota Regiments, support for families of soldiers, letters soldiers sent to the governor, procurement of equipment and supplies, the Dakota Conflict, conditions affecting Minnesotans in Confederate prison camps, reports of sick and wounded from Minnesota regiments, correspondence with federal military and civilian officials. Non military topics are also included in this series. Such issues as financing railroads and encouraging immigration also find their way into the Governor's Records.

- *Executive Journals, 1858 - 1915,* include copies of official acts, appointments, pardons, messages to the Minnesota legislature as well as communications to and from the national government. Especially interesting are letters and telegrams to the War Department, Secretary of War and Adjutant General of the United States relating to Minnesota's role in the war effort. The series now in the state archives at the MHS also includes letters from the governor to officers commanding Minnesota regiments and reports from those units to the governor. Some have been published and can be found in libraries or rare book stores.

- *Annual and Biennial Reports, 1860-1924* from the Adjutant General's office are held by the MHS. These reports provide extensive information on military events involving Minnesotans from territorial days (1860 report) through 1924. Each report includes a statement from the Adjutant General and many pages of appendices containing rosters, muster rolls, supply and ordnance lists, casualty lists, general and special orders, and statistics concerning pensions, arrears in pay, and other claims.

  Reports were also required by the U.S. Congress for federal programs operating in Minnesota, including the Office of Indian Affairs. These reports were published in serial sets, and are also available at the MHS Library and other libraries. The Library of Congress has made some of them available on the internet on their American Memory pages under the term "A Century of Lawmaking for a New Nation" at <http://memory.loc.gov/>.

- *U.S. War Department, Commissary General of Subsistence, Minnesota District. Records, 1859-1874.* Copied from RG 192 at the National Archives, this record set includes detailed requests and expenditures for supplies used by U.S. troops stationed on the Minnesota and Dakota Territory frontier during the Dakota Conflict and the Civil War as well as expenditures at Fort Snelling. These are also available at the MHS Library, manuscript file number P1448.

Pensions

Three principal types of pensions were provided to servicemen and their families. **Disability pensions** were awarded for physical disabilities which occurred in the line of duty. **Service pensions** were awarded to veterans who served for specific periods of time. **Widows' pensions** were awarded to women and children whose husbands or fathers had been killed or who had served for specific periods of time.

Numerous acts of Congress from 14 July of 1862 through 1 May 1920 authorized the payment of pensions to large classes of veterans or dependents who met certain eligibility criteria. In addition to the various pension acts, some pensions were awarded to specific persons who merited consideration, but who would not be eligible otherwise. For example, **parents** who were dependent on a son for support were sometimes awarded pensions. These are typically noted in the U.S. Serial Set.

- **Federal pension application files** include basic information on the identity of the claimant, his service, and evidence of the action taken by the government. If a widow applied, her application was filed under the veteran's name. A typical application would include at least: name, rank, military unit, period of service, residence, birthplace, date of birth or age. A widow's application would include most of those facts, plus similar information on her, including maiden name, marriage date and place, and her spouse's death date and place. A child's or heir's application would include all of that plus the names of all heirs, dates and places of their births, and the date of their mother's death. The files often include supporting documents, such as discharge papers, affidavits and depositions of witnesses, narratives of service which would indicate participation, marriage certificates, records of medical expenses, pages from family Bibles, and other papers. Copies of Federal pension application files can be ordered on-line or through the mail using Form NATF 85. If you are sure you have the right person, it is best to order the entire file, and not the abridged file.

Federal pension index card showing Montgomery's service in Co. K, 7th Minnesota and in the US Colored Infantry, with the casefile numbers for both him and his widow, Sarah.

Be aware that the Veterans Administration still holds some files for widows and others who drew pensions after 1930.

The National Archives has released a series of microfilms which index the pension files they hold for Civil War veterans:

- *General Index to Pension Files, 1861-1934*, National Archives Microfilm T288 – 544 rolls. The cards provide the name of the veteran, name and class of dependent, if any, service data, application/file number, and for approved claims, pension number and state from which the claim was filed. Subscribers to <Ancestry.com> can access the index and images of the cards as well.

- *Organization Index to Pension Files of Veterans Who Served Between 1861 and 1900. T289. 765 rolls. 16mm.* [rolls 1-400] Minnesota is on reels 251-256. The information provided here is virtually the same as that in the *General Index to Pension Files, 1861-1934, T288*, listed above. Unlike the alphabetical *General Index*, however, this index groups the applicants according to the units in which they served. The cards are arranged alphabetically by state, then by arm of service (infantry, cavalry, artillery), then numerically by regiment, and then alphabetically by veteran's surname.

Roll	Unit
251	Co. A, 1 Minn. Inf.— McCullochm - Co. I, 3 Minn. Inf.
252	Co. K, 3 Minn. Inf.— Co. B, 7 Minn. Inf.
253	Co. C, 7 Minn. Inf.— Co. F, 11 Minn. Inf.
254	Co. G, 11 Minn. Inf.— Co. I, 14 Minn. Inf. (SAW)
255	Co. K, 14 Minn. Inf. (SAW)— Co. E, Hatch's Bn., Minn. Cav.
256	Co. F, Hatch's Bn., Minn. Cav.— Co. D, 6 Miss. Inf.

The State of Minnesota also awarded pensions and provided services to military veterans and/or dependents, and administered payment of Federal pensions. These records are held in the state archives at the MHS.

- The *Minnesota Adjutant General's Office Pension Registers*, held by MHS, cover veterans of military service who resided in Minnesota at the time the claim was made, regardless of the state from which they served. They cover the period from about 1878 to 1949. Organized by the date the claim was filed, the records list type of claim (e.g., original, arrears, increase, restoration, widow, etc.), claimant's name, address, military unit and rank, information to support claim, action on claim. Widows or children of servicemen filed many of the applications. The registers provide claimant's name (alphabetized by the first two letters of the surname) and the page number(s).

A card index to these pension files and more can be found in the Weyerhaeuser Reading Room at the MHS Library. It is a compilation of data gathered from various sources, including Grand Army of the Republic (GAR) encampment proceedings, death date, and residence within Minnesota. Many of the cards are for veterans who did *not* serve in Minnesota regiments, but who moved to the state following their service. Note that the beginning date is 1878. Some veterans and/or dependents living in Minnesota began receiving pensions before that date or dealt directly with the Pension Office in Washington, DC. Their pensions will not appear in this index. (Family historians often find that different sources may have different information, and it can all be accurate!)

The index cards are easy to use: in this example, Chas. W. Woolford served as a musician in Company A of the 35th New York Infantry. He was age 65 in 1904, died in May of 1925, and his widow Gertrude A. was eligible for a widow's

```
Woodford, Chas. W
           Gertrude A
35 N.Y. A           musician
                65 in '04       G:164
5/14/25                         G:253
at Lake City                    U:44
        "        in '09    Y:223   A2:411
St. Paul GAR               P:168
S.H. in '10
St. Paul in '05
```

pension. The entries on the right hand side of the card refer to pages in the Minnesota Adjutant General's Pension Registers in the State Archives. With this information, you can find the pages in the set of Registers. If your ancestor lived in Minnesota, even if his service was not in a Minnesota regiment, this card file might provide additional information for you.

- The *Minnesota Adjutant General's Office Indian War Pension Registers* (1905-1937) list claims filed by persons who performed military or relief services during the Dakota Conflict of 1862, under an act of the state legislature of 19 April 1905. This act provided for a pension of up to $12 per month for Minnesota residents who were not already drawing a U.S. or Minnesota pension and who "rendered active service, bore arms, or otherwise render efficient aid and suffered any disabilities in the Indian massacre of 1862." There are separate index volumes to accompany the registers.

The information in the *Registers* includes claim number, date filed, claimant's name, residence, service unit and rank, injury or health problem claims, date the claims was allowed or the date and reason it was rejected, amount of monthly payment, the payment authorization number, age at time of application, and a narrative, sometimes lengthy, of proof of service and/or health problem in support of the claim. The death date of the pension was usually added later.

- *Minnesota Adjutant General's Office Indian War Pension Files* (1905-ca. 1950) include a variety of documents, such as application forms, affidavits of service, marriage and death certificates and sometimes Civil War discharge papers. There is an alphabetical index in the Minnesota Historical Society Library.

The Minnesota Department of Veterans Affairs administers state-sponsored programs for those who served in either federal service or in the Minnesota National Guard or Militia. The following sets of records are available through the State Archives at the Minnesota Historical Society Library.

- *Minnesota Soldiers Home (Minneapolis), Relief Records, 1905-1965*. Records of relief payments to veterans of the Civil War, the Spanish-American War, and World War I, or their survivors, and including biographical data (1905-1934); other scattered records on relief applications (1940s-1965); and receipt books (1929-1932) and monthly reports (1959-1961) of the Woman's Relief Corps.

  The main set of relief record books gives, for each recipient, name, address, spouse's name and service data, income and disability information, living arrangements, amount of pension, and a record of pension payments. Some of the records are indexed, but not all.

- There are also resident and administrative records for the state-operated *Minnesota Veterans Home* in Minneapolis (established 1887), including admission and discharge records, histories of residents' military service, hospital and clinic records, and population reports, plus administrative records held by the Minnesota Historical Society. When first established, this institution served as a charity hospital, and not as a home for the elderly as it is today. Veterans could be admitted multiple times for stays of a few weeks or months, and then return to their homes.

- *Veterans' Graves Registrations*. These records provide information on the branch of service, unit, cause of death, place of burial and other biographical information. From 1930 to 1975, funeral directors or the county veterans service officer were asked to fill out a form. The forms are arranged by county and chronologically with a separate section for Ft. Snelling National Cemetery. The Minnesota Historical Society website links to an on-line index.

- *Minnesota Board of Auditors for the Adjustment of Claims for War Expenditures Records, 1862-1868*. There were three boards of auditors so named, all established by the legislature to settle claims of private persons for compensation for services rendered during the Dakota War, 1862.

  The ledgers include the minutes of the meetings established to identify how claims were to be filed, what constituted proof of claim, and where the auditors would travel to take testimony on them. Entries are by date,

A Genealogist's Guide to Researching Civil War and Dakota Conflict Ancestors in Minnesota

then claim number. These are particularly interesting, because they include non-military personnel such as teamsters, farmers who provided stabling, ferrymen who transported troops, etc. With the difficulty in getting usable supplies from St. Paul to the upper Minnesota River valley, horses as well as men were impressed into service. The records are held in the Minnesota State Archives at the Minnesota Historical Society and are unindexed.

The 1003 claims of the first board, which met from September-December 1862, have been extracted and published by Park Genealogical Books as *Claims from the Dakota Conflict: Supplying the Local Militia– Volume 1: October- November 1862.*

From the first ledger of the Minnesota Board of Auditors for the Adjustment of Claims for War Expenditures.

- There are case files for Minnesota military claims in the National Archives, RG 217, Records of the Accounting Officers of the Department of the Treasury.

Compiling a Soldier's Record

You will need to compile information on your ancestor's service for your family history from military and other sources. This step can lead to further research and questions which you will likely want to pursue. The following case study can illustrate this best.

The last surviving veteran of the Civil War, Albert Woolson, died in Duluth, Minnesota in 1956 at age 109. Woolson served as a musician in the First Minnesota Heavy Artillery Regiment. He was a fixture at many GAR encampments (reunions) and was well known around the state. The GAR monument at Gettysburg shows Woolson seated in a chair (and a duplicate of the statue is on display in Duluth). The Biography Card File at the Minnesota Historical Society Library lists extensive obituaries for him, with many photos taken throughout his long life. He is, perhaps, one of the most written about privates who served in the Civil War. However, compiling data for him illustrates why a family researcher needs to be persistent in the search.

Because one of his sons was given his name and also lived in Minnesota, two Albert Woolsons appear in some census indexes. Additional information is needed to separate their data. As one is father, born 1848, and the other son, born 1878, their dates of birth can be used to separate them for both the Soundex (phonetic) indexes of 1900 and 1920 and the on-line indexes. However, the on-line census indexes for 1910 and 1930 do *not* include Albert, the father, in any state. Applying the normal life expectancy could lead to the mistaken thought that Albert died after the 1920 census was taken, and before the 1930 census was taken. His death date is actually 2 August 1956, age 109.

Albert Woolson (First_Last)
Regiment Name 1 Minn. Heavy Artillery
Side Union
Company ? | C,D
Soldier's Rank_In ? | Musn.
Soldier's Rank_Out ? | Pvt.
Alternate Name ? | Albert/Wolson
Notes
Film Number M546 roll 10

Woolson's record from the Soldiers & Sailors System.

```
                              '90 Mankato

Woolson, Albert
1 Minn. H.A. D /
                       b. 2/11/48 in New York
Duluth in '06
```

Woolson's card in the MHS Civil War Index, which does not show his pension information.

Woolson's pension card from the National Archives microfilm.

According to his card in the MHS Civil War Index, Albert moved to Duluth, Minnesota, in 1906, and died there in 1956. A check in the Duluth City Directories for 1910 and 1930 show that he *is* in fact living there. He does not appear in the on-line indexes perhaps because he is not a head-of-household; that is, he is living with one of his children. To find his census record, it is necessary to look up his address from the city directory on a census map, and then search that area of Duluth in the census.

Note also that his National Archives pension card indicates that he applied for and received his military pension as a Minnesota resident, and yet that information does not appear on the Minnesota Historical Society index card.

Yet this is just part of Woolson's story. The puzzle pieces needed for his story come from a variety of sources. Copies of his military record and pension file can be obtained through the National Archives. Copies of his enlistment and regimental records can be obtained through MHS. His participation in the GAR is documented in its published *Proceedings* [see page 52]. Coverage of his funeral attracted dignitaries from all parts of the U.S., with a fly-over by the Duluth Air Wing, and required almost four full pages in the *Duluth Herald*. His very interesting biographical information can be found in various newspapers in the Minnesota Historical Society collection including those published in the Twin Cities, and local sources in Duluth.

What can you learn about your ancestor's life?

Second, Research the Unit

While the resources here may not mention a specific soldier by name, they provide a sense of what an individual experienced while a member of the unit. Unit histories can be as personal as one written by a private in a particular company or by an officer of a regiment, or as broad as a listing of the service provided by that entire company.

- *Minnesota in the Civil and Indian Wars: Volume II* (St. Paul: Minnesota Board of Commissions on Publication of History of Minnesota in Civil and Indian Wars, 1890-1893) reproduces many of the official reports and correspondence of Minnesota units. It supplements those found in the next source, which also contains references to Minnesota units in the reports of other state regiments. The Dakota Conflict coverage is broader and more organized in this reference than it is in the next.

- U.S. War Department. *War of the Rebellion: A Compilation of the Official Records of the Union and Confederate Armies*. 128 vols. Washington, DC: Government Printing Office, 1880-1900. Reprint, Gettysburg, PA: National Historical Society, 1971-72. Commonly known as Official Records or "The OR" this set includes battle reports and correspondence of Union and Confederate regiments. Scans of the actual pages with a search engine is available at the Making of America site <http://library 5.library.cornell.edu/moa/moa_browse.html>.

Another set covers Naval war records. Both the Army and Naval sets can be found at the MHS Library.

Although there is a separate General Index volume to the OR, it is incomplete and somewhat difficult to use. Anyone undertaking extensive research in the Official Records should consult *A Users' Guide to the Official Records of the American Civil War* by Alan C. and Barbara A. Aimone (Shippensburg, PA: White Mane Publishing, 1993). This provides an excellent overview of the creation and history of the OR, its organization and limitations. It also includes some useful appendices correlating events to specific volumes and to other sources. The Guild Press CD includes the Aimone reference, plus the Dyer and Fox resources listed below.

248   MO., ARK., KANS., IND. T., AND DEPT. N. W.   [CHAP. XXV.

AUGUST 20-22, 1862.—Actions with Indians at Fort Ridgely, Minn.

REPORTS.

No. 1.—Lieut. Timothy J. Sheehan, Fifth Minnesota Infantry.
No. 2.—Ordnance Sergt. John Jones, U. S. Army.

No 1.

Report of Lieut. Timothy J. Sheehan, Fifth Minnesota Infantry.

HEADQUARTERS FORT RIDGELY, MINN.,
August 26, 1862.

GENERAL: I have the honor to report that this post was assaulted by a large force of Sioux Indians on the 20th instant. The small remnant of Company B, Fifth Regiment Minnesota Volunteers, together with a detachment of Company C, Fifth Regiment Minnesota Volunteers, and the Renville Rangers, a company just organized for one of the regiments of this State, were the only troops I had under my command for its defense, and nobly did they do their duty. The engagement lasted until dusk, when the Indians, finding that they could not effect a lodgment, which was prevented in a great measure by the superior fire of the artillery, under the immediate charge of Ordnance Sergt. J. Jones, U. S. Army, which compelled them to evacuate the ravines by which this post is surrounded, withdrew their forces, and the gallant little garrison rested on their arms, ready for any attack.

During the night several people, remnants of once thriving families, arrived at the post in a most miserable condition, some wounded—severely burned—having made their escape from their dwellings, which were fired by the Indians. The people in the immediate vicinity fled to the post for protection, and were organized and armed, as far as practicable, to aid in the defense.

On the 22d they returned with a much larger force and attacked us on all sides, but the most determined was on the east and west corners of the fort, which are in the immediate vicinity of ravines. The west corner was also covered by stables and log buildings, which afforded the Indians great protection, and, in order to protect the garrison, I ordered them to be destroyed. Some were fired by the artillery, and the balance by the Renville Rangers, under the command of First Lieut. J. Gorman, to whom, and the men under his command, great credit is due for their gallant conduct. The balls fell thick all over and through the wooden building erected for officers' quarters. Still the men maintained their ground. The Indians prepared to storm, but the gallant conduct of the men at the guns paralyzed them, and compelled them to withdraw, after one of the most determined attacks ever made by Indians on a military post.

The men of Companies B and C, Fifth Regiment Minnesota Volunteers, aided by citizens, did good execution, and deserve the highest praise for their heroic conduct.

I beg leave also to bring to your notice Dr. Muller, the acting assistant surgeon of this post, who, assisted by his excellent lady, attended the wounded promptly; and I am happy to say that, under his careful treatment, most all of them are prospering favorably. Mr. Wykoff and party, of the Indian Department, with many other citizens, rendered efficient service.

Our small-arms ammunition nearly failing, on consultation with

Part of Lt. Sheehan's official report from the Dakota attack on Fort Ridgely, as printed in the *Official Records*.

- *Atlas to Accompany the Official Records of the Union and Confederate Armies 1891*, reprinted as *The Official Military Atlas of the Civil War* in 1983 – is a compilation of maps produced during the War, featuring more than 800 maps plus an index to those in the first 53 volumes of the OR. The reprint includes illustrations of the uniforms worn by different units and ranks.

- *Compiled Records Showing Service of Military Units in Volunteer Union Organizations*. Beginning in 1890, the War Department compiled histories of the volunteer military organizations that served during the Civil War. The compiled records for each organization are in jacket-envelopes bearing the title "Record of Events" and giving the name of the unit. Many of the envelopes contain abstracts of the information found in the record-of-events section of the original muster rolls and returns. Also included are some cards showing the exact captions of the muster-in and muster-out rolls and the certifications by the mustering officers verifying the accuracy of the rolls. The jacket-envelopes for a few units contain no documents but only references to other units with which these units were merged.

  Compiled service histories contain no information about individual soldiers. The abstracts instead relate to the stations, movements, or activities of each unit or part of it. Frequently there is information about the unit's organization or composition, strength and losses, and disbandment. Sometimes the cards also show the names of commanding officers, the dates the unit was mustered into service and mustered out, the terms of service, and similar information.

  The data is taken from Record Groups 94 and 407 at the National Archives, which also produced a descriptive pamphlet of the contents of the set (M594–225 rolls). The MHS Library has those referring to Minnesota units, filed as M515.

- *Returns from United States Military Posts, 1800-1916* are monthly returns of most military posts, camps, and stations, generally showing units that were present, their strength, names and duties of officers, numbers of officers present and absent, and a record of events. They have been microfilmed by the National Archives as M617 – 1550 reels. The MHS Library has those reels generally relating to Minnesota and surrounding territories and states. These include locations such as Fort Snelling, Fort Ridgley, etc. as well as lesser outposts on the frontier. This series also includes reports from troops stationed at Mankato. Much of the information relates to the Dakota Conflict. The 27-reel series at MHS is filed as M195.

- The *Medical and Surgical History of the Civil War*, prepared by Surgeon General Joseph K. Barnes, 1870 (reprinted by Broadfoot 1991; originally titled *Medical and Surgical History of the War of the Rebellion 1861-1865* and published by the Superintendent of Documents in Washington, DC) contains twelve volumes of illustrated medical case studies of wounds and diseases. It was compiled by the Surgeon General from information collected from the military hospitals during the Civil War and describes treatment methods and techniques. The MHS and other libraries hold either the six-volume original set or the twelve-volume reprint. The reprint includes an index volume, while the original volumes are indexed separately. This set can help you determine the treatment your wounded ancestor may have received, and understand the medical reasons for his pension.

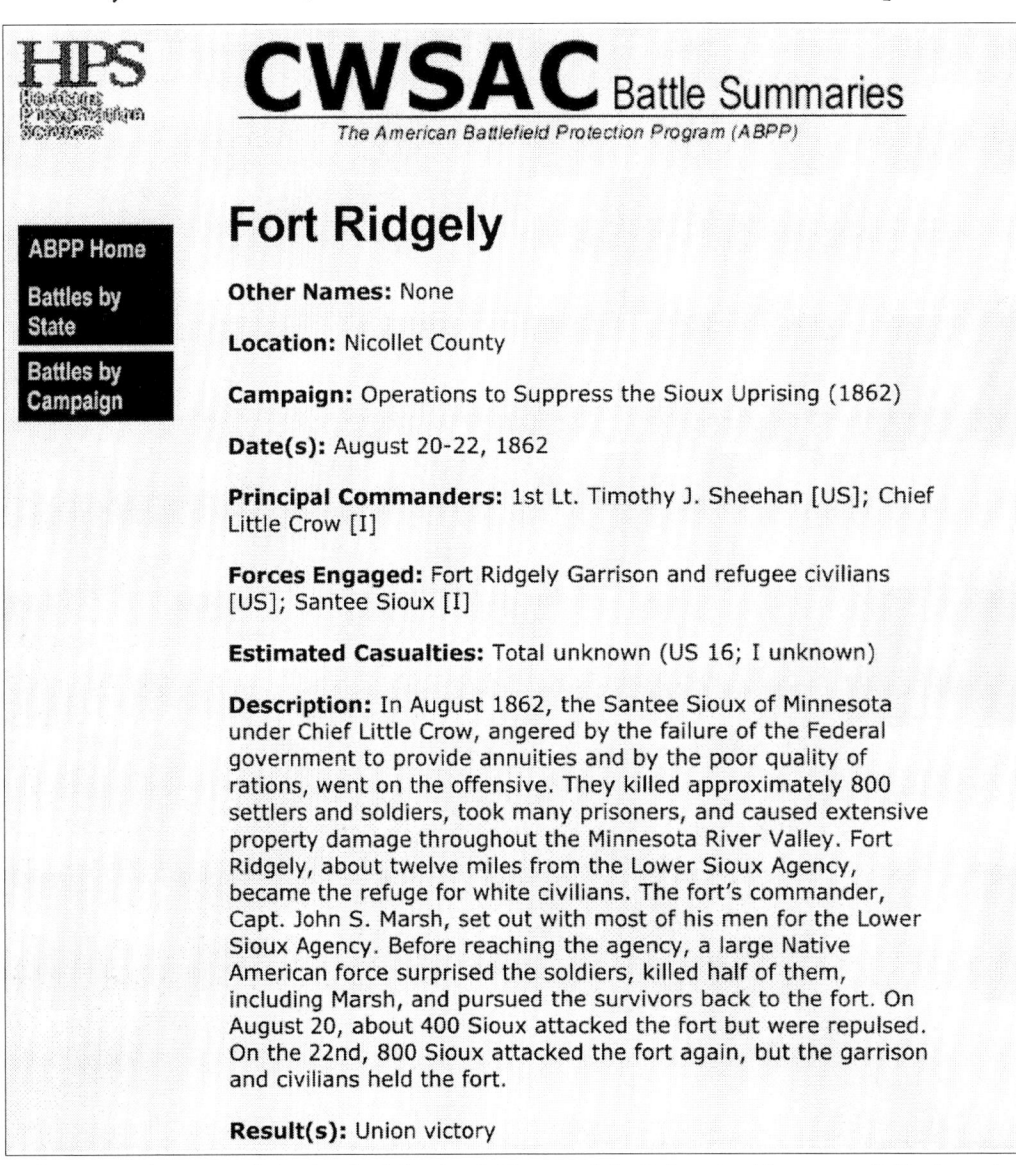

HPS Historic Preservation Services

CWSAC Battle Summaries
The American Battlefield Protection Program (ABPP)

ABPP Home
Battles by State
Battles by Campaign

Fort Ridgely

Other Names: None

Location: Nicollet County

Campaign: Operations to Suppress the Sioux Uprising (1862)

Date(s): August 20-22, 1862

Principal Commanders: 1st Lt. Timothy J. Sheehan [US]; Chief Little Crow [I]

Forces Engaged: Fort Ridgely Garrison and refugee civilians [US]; Santee Sioux [I]

Estimated Casualties: Total unknown (US 16; I unknown)

Description: In August 1862, the Santee Sioux of Minnesota under Chief Little Crow, angered by the failure of the Federal government to provide annuities and by the poor quality of rations, went on the offensive. They killed approximately 800 settlers and soldiers, took many prisoners, and caused extensive property damage throughout the Minnesota River Valley. Fort Ridgely, about twelve miles from the Lower Sioux Agency, became the refuge for white civilians. The fort's commander, Capt. John S. Marsh, set out with most of his men for the Lower Sioux Agency. Before reaching the agency, a large Native American force surprised the soldiers, killed half of them, including Marsh, and pursued the survivors back to the fort. On August 20, about 400 Sioux attacked the fort but were repulsed. On the 22nd, 800 Sioux attacked the fort again, but the garrison and civilians held the fort.

Result(s): Union victory

Information about specific battles, both for the Civil War and the Dakota Conflict, are available through the National Park Service's Soldiers & Sailors System. Note that only those battles in which regular military troops fought are included.

General References

The following resources are available in print at many libraries, including the Minnesota Historical Society, and were compiled from resources in the National Archives. They are searchable on-line through the NPS Civil War Soldiers & Sailors System. The Dyer and Fox resources are also bundled with the OR on the Guild Press CD.

- Dyer, Frederick H. *A Compendium of the War of the Rebellion*. Des Moines, IA: Dyer Publishing Co., 1908. Reprint, Dayton, OH: National Historical Society, 1979. Lists battles and campaigns for Union regiments and also gives the composition of corps and armies, i.e., such as the Army of the Potomac.

- Fox, William F. *Regimental Losses in the American Civil War 1861-1865: A Treatise on the Extent and Nature of the Mortuary Losses in the United States*... Albany, NY: Albany Publishing Company, 1889. This includes most of the regiments in Federal service, the U.S Colored Troops and some Confederate regiments.

- The National Park Service's *Soldiers & Sailors System* includes battle summaries. The guerilla tactics used by the Dakota Indians and the amount of time required to move regular Army troops into position resulted in few actual battles during the conflict. For example, New Ulm (Brown County) was attacked on two separate occasions, but only militia were available for defense, not regular troops. Therefore, New Ulm does not appear as a battlefield in the database.

Minnesota References

Interest in the Civil War has resulted in many books about battles, campaigns, military leaders, or particular units and soldiers. Check the catalogs at all the repositories you visit for specific histories. Both reprints and new works are available.

- **Eye-witness accounts and reminiscences** from the Dakota Conflict of 1862 can be found in published works, newspapers, letters, diaries, and other manuscripts. The Minnesota Historical Society has gathered many of the manuscripts together into one 4-reel series of microfilm, entitled *Dakota Conflict of 1862 Manuscript Collection*, M582. Sources include soldiers and civilians as well as both Indian and white participants. They are individually identified on the MHS on-line catalog.

  In addition, there are many pamphlets and newspaper articles detailing personal experiences, including some written by those who had been held captive by the Indians. On-line library catalogs and the National Union

Catalog for Manuscript Collections (see page 25) can be helpful in finding some of these scattered resources.

- Baker, Robert Orr, *The Muster Roll: A Biography of Fort Ripley, Minnesota*, St. Paul: H.M. Smythe and Co., 19--. This well documented history of the fort includes its role in the story of Hole-in-the-Day and the possibility of the Ojibway joining the Dakota in 1862.

- Beck, Paul N. *Soldiers, Settlers and Sioux: Fort Ridgely and the Minnesota River Valley, 1853-1867*, Sioux Falls, South Dakota: Center for Western Studies, 2000. A history of this Fort, prominent in the Spirit Lake Uprising in 1857 as well as the 1862 Dakota Conflict.

- Bergemann, Kurt, *Brackett's Battalion*, St. Paul: MHS Press, 2004. This cavalry unit served in both the war against the Confederacy and against the Dakota Indians, becoming seasoned/battle-hardened troops very quickly. It's a fascinating story!

- Bircher, William. *A Drummer-Boy's Diary: Comprising four years service with the Second Regiment Minnesota Veteran Volunteers, 1861-1865*. St. Cloud, Minnesota: North Star Press, 1995.

- Bishop, Judson Wade. *The Story of a Regiment, Being a Narrative of the Service of the Second Regiment Minnesota Veteran Volunteer Infantry, 1861-1865*. 1890, reprint now available from North Star Press, Newell Chester, editor. Photos and biographical sketches of key people were added for the reprint, North Star Press, 2000.

- Brown, Alonzo L. *History of the Fourth Regiment of Minnesota Infantry Volunteers during the Great Rebellion, 1861-1865*. St. Paul, Minn.: Pioneer Press Co., 1892. This volume has been reprinted by Higginson Book Company, Salem, Mass.

- Dornbusch, Charles Emil, compiler. *Regimental Publications & Personal Narratives of the Civil War: A Checklist*. New York: New York Public Library, 1961-[1972]. This set covers the entire U.S. and is available in many libraries. Your local public library may be able to get copies of publications for you through interlibrary loan.

- Folwell, William Watts. *History of Minnesota*, St. Paul: Minnesota Historical Society, 1969 (revised). In four volumes, the second includes excellent information about this time period.

- Heard, I.V.D. *History of the Sioux War*. Originally published in 1866, and often included with other local histories. Heard served as recording secretary for the trials of the Dakota Indian, and therefore had first-hand knowledge.

- Leehan, Brian, *Pale Horse at Plum Run: the First Minnesota at Gettysburg*, St. Paul: Minnesota Historical Society Press, 2002. Includes a bibliography and index.

- Moe, Richard. *The Last Full Measure: the Life and Death of the First Minnesota Volunteers.* St. Paul: MHS, 1993. The authoritative work.

- Neill, E.D., *History of the Minnesota Valley*, Minneapolis, Minnesota: North Star Publishing Co., 1882. This volume includes Heard's work, plus county histories with biographies along the Minnesota River. It's been reprinted several times, and is now available on CD as well.

- Powell, William H. (William Henry), 1838-1901 comp. *List of officers of the Army of the United States from 1779 to 1900, Embracing a Register of all Appointments by the President of the United States in the Volunteer Service During the Civil War, and of Volunteer Officers in the Service of the United States. June 1, 1900.* Comp. from the official records by Colonel Wm. H. Powell. New York: L. R. Hamersly & Co., 1900. Useful for those who were commissioned as officers, i.e., above Lieutenant.

- Satterlee, Marion, *Outbreak and Massacre by the Dakota Indians in Minnesota in 1862*, reprint Bowie, Maryland: Heritage Books, 2001. This amateur historian sought out survivors and descendants to compile the lists of victims, prisoners, refugees, Indians killed in battle and hanged, and those pardoned at Rock Island. There are also reports of attacks on individual settlers and battles fought with the military. He published several versions: this appears to be the 1925 version of his work.

- Woolworth, Alan and Bakeman, Mary, *With Camera and Sketchbook*, Roseville, Minnesota: Park Genealogical Books, 2004. Reprint of the eyewitness account by one of the first photojournalists, Adrian J. Ebell (who served on Col. Sibley's staff), and accompanied by drawings by his comrade Albert Colgrave. It includes an annotated list of the dead at Birch Coolie.

- The *Civil War Portal* <http://www.civilwarportal.com> provides a series of links to various internet sites that may be of interest to researchers. They include general resources, military officers, battles and campaigns, etc.

- The *American Civil War Homepage* at <http://sunsite.utk.edu/civil-war/warweb.html> includes a series of links to internet sites, including music, biographical information on war leaders, images of wartime, general resources, battles and campaigns, Civil War Roundtables, re-enactments, etc.

Civilians at Home

Researching civilians at home in Minnesota can be a challenge because of the Dakota Conflict. Settlers had been pouring into the Minnesota River valley in the early 1860s, and had lived in peace with the Dakota. It is difficult to know just how many arrived after the taking of the 1860 census, but before the beginning of the conflict in August 1862. The six weeks of conflict changed everything: some settlers fled, never to return; some were massacred in their cabins and fields. As steps were taken to remove the Dakota Indians from Minnesota, settlers again came though more slowly to the southwestern part of the state.

The Press

Minnesota residents received news about the war from the local press as well as news magazines printed in the east, such as *Harper's Weekly* and *Frank Leslie's Illustrated Newspaper*, which provided wonderful sketches of the action. Eastern newspapers, such as the *New York Times*, were shipped in. They published articles about the Dakota Conflict as well as reporting on the Civil War. Many of the newspapers in the area along the Minnesota River were published weekly; those in major metropolitan areas were published several times per week, or even daily.

Local newspapers chronicle local stories, and can provide insight into the issues of the day. Communities such as St. Paul, St. Peter, Shakopee and Mankato had multiple newspapers, favoring different political points of view. Some articles were copied from other papers, such as reports of officers and battle reports. In addition to announcements of local birth, marriages and deaths before the advent of governmental vital records in the state, newspapers printed letters from the local soldiers, reported on the comings and goings of the troops, and the opinions of dignitaries such as Bishop Whipple or Senator Rice or others. Unlike more modern wars, there was no censorship, and no military authority opened or read the letters home. A soldier could tell the local newspaper or the family exactly what he thought about life in the Army. Some letters contained detailed accounts of military operations, something that would not be permitted today.

The Minnesota Historical Society (MHS) has collected the state's newspapers since its inception in 1849. They are available to researchers at the MHS Library and through interlibrary loan to other libraries.

Refugee Relief

From the beginning of the Dakota conflict, settlers from the Minnesota River valley became refugees as they fled the possibility of attack. The Legislature quickly established a Commission and a fund for their relief. The fund received contributions from Boston, Philadelphia and other large cities as the word spread. The Legislative Report of the Minnesota State Commissioner for the Distribution of the Refugee Fund from 28 February 1863 has been published in the *Minnesota Genealogical Journal: 30*, available in some libraries or from Park Genealogical Books [see page 57].

Grand Army of the Republic, Department of Minnesota

The Grand Army of the Republic (GAR) was a patriotic society, founded in 1866, composed of Civil War veterans who had served honorably in the Union Army. This society was dissolved in 1956 (in Minnesota in 1954), with the death of its last surviving member. Since the GAR was a private veterans organization, not a part of the Federal Government, its archives are not among the records in the National Archives. Records of the Minnesota Department can be found at MHS.

- *General administrative records* of the headquarters office, include correspondence, Minnesota encampment proceedings (1900-1947), a partial set of financial records, death lists and reports on members, miscellaneous data on GAR posts, and an assortment of printed memorabilia. The death lists have been compiled and published.

- *Roll of the Dead, 1886-1906, Minnesota Grand Army of the Republic*, compiled by Antona Richardson and published by Paduan Press, provides an alphabetic roster with more than 3100 deceased members of the GAR, with the date of death and name and Minnesota location of the Post to which they belonged. Beginning in 1894, military rank in Minnesota or other-state unit in which they served, day and month of death, and for some, cause of death are also reported. The information was transcribed from the yearly *Journal of the Proceedings of the Annual Encampment of the Minnesota Department of the Grand Army of the Republic*.

Also included in the GAR materials are records of the Woman's Veteran Relief Union (1900-1910) and the Woman's Relief Corps (1884-1948); and smaller files regarding the Military Order of the Loyal Legion (1913-1920), the Past National Aide Club (1935-1944), the Memorial Day Association (1917-1953), and other affiliates.

- The *Woman's Relief Corps* or WRC (1884-1948) was the auxiliary organization of the GAR. Their delegates to the encampments for 1886-1895 (with place of residence) have been compiled and published in the *Minnesota Genealogical Journal: 26*, September 2001 [see page 57 for information on ordering back issues], and some limited information on deaths for 1905 and officers in 1906 in the *Minnesota Genealogist*, Vol. 21, issues 2 and 4. The *Minnesota Genealogist* is the quarterly journal of the Minnesota Genealogical Society.

- The *Military Order of the Loyal Legion of the United States* (MOLLUS) was organized by former officers in the Union Army. Various state chapters published reports of their annual meetings which included biographical information, obituaries, and published versions of addresses given by members. These often took the form of personal accounts of actions or campaigns in which the individual served. The Minnesota chapter of MOLLUS collected and published a separate series under the title *Glimpses of the Nation's Struggle*. This series is available at the Minnesota Historical Society Library and other libraries. Broadfoot has reprinted the entire series. There are some Minnesota accounts in materials from other states, too.

- Some *GAR Post Records*, including minute books, registers of members, dues ledgers etc. are in the collections at MHS, though rather difficult to use. Some of them are available on microfilm through the Family History Libraries as well. Check the on-line catalog at <www.familysearch.org>. Records for Acker Post No. 21 (St. Paul) and Bryant Post No. 119 (Minneapolis) are two of the more than 70 posts whose partial records have been microfilmed by MHS, and are available to public libraries on interlibrary loan. Published directories and additional post records can be found at county and local historical societies and public libraries throughout the state.

Depredation Claims

The Dakota Conflict resulted in much loss of life, injury to individuals, capture of women and children, and extensive loss of property. An act of Congress of February 16, 1863 for the relief of Minnesota residents who suffered damage and injury authorized the payment of $200,000 from the annuities due the Sioux, and the appointment of three commissions to ascertain the entire amount of damages and the persons eligible to participate. About 2600 claims were filed, for a total of more than $1.3 million in damages. They are listed in *Index to Claimants for Depredations following the Dakota War of 1862*, compiled by Mary Bakeman, Roseville, Minnesota: Park Genealogical Books, 2001.

Approximately 525 case files in support of the claims are in RG 75 at the National Archives, with copies at Park Genealogical Books that can be purchased. They include affidavits of claimants on the circumstances justifying the claim, the property lost and its value, and often information on the claimant's family. Transcripts of testimony by witnesses and others in support of the claimant are also included. A list of the names of those whose casefiles exist can be found in the *Minnesota Genealogical Journal: 21*, March 1999 or on the internet at
<http://www.parkbooks.com/Html/res_depd.html>.

Travel

Planning a vacation or two around the military service of your ancestor can be lots of fun. Because you have already gathered the information on where the unit served, it's a relatively simple matter to check out the battlefields for the units and plan a virtual trip or an actual one.

The National Parks System includes many of the battlefields and national cemeteries. Its website at <http://cwar.nps.gov/civilwar/> is full of information helpful to travelers on what to see and do. In addition, it provides a great deal of background information about the war, such as timelines, battles, stories, etc. at <http://cwar.nps.gov/civilwar/aboutcivwar.html>. The sites include several in Minnesota, such as Fort Ridgely and Wood Lake, where federal troops were involved in the Dakota Conflict.

A virtual tour of Gettysburg produced by the National Parks Service is available at <http://www.nps.gov/gett/getttour/main-ms.htl>. It is impressive! A google search for the battles in which you are interested is likely to offer additional possibilities.

The Minnesota Historical Society has established historical sites along the Minnesota River. Some communities (such as New Ulm and Mankato) have monuments memorializing the Dakota Conflict. A trip to the Twin Cities should include a visit to Historic Fort Snelling, built at the confluence of the Minnesota and Mississippi Rivers and the training ground for Minnesota's Civil War regiments. Details for for sites along the Minnesota River can be found at <http://www.exploreminnesota.com/minnesota_river_valley.html> (all one line).

Combining your family research with visits to these places is appealing to the entire family.

The entry to Historic Fort Snelling, St. Paul.

Contact Information

Reprints of the individual regimental histories and rosters from *Minnesota in the Civil and Indian Wars* and the *Index to the Adjutant General's Report of 1866* are available from Park Genealogical Books, as are other resources for family history research in Minnesota during the Civil War era.check us out on the web at
<http://www.parkbooks.com/>

The *Minnesota Genealogical Journal* is published by Park Genealogical Books semi-annually in March and September and is available by subscription. Back issues are also available. Details can be found on

<http://www.parkbooks.com/Html/mgjbroch.html>

For a full contents listing by issue, see

<http://www.parkbooks.com/Html/mgjpast.html>

Write to us at
Park Genealogical Books
P O Box 130968
Roseville, MN 55113